The Portobello Cookbook

by
Ron Meyer

To Betsy
Good
Eating
[signature]

ISBN 0-9671074-0-7

Published by Jared March Publishing Group
714 West Bay Avenue
Barnegat, NJ 08005

Printed by Morris Press, Kearney Nebraska

Dedication

*With special thanks to Chef Ray Cetrulo of **I Fratelli Restaurant** in Bloomfield, New Jersey (973-338-4888) whose wisdom and knowledge is always an inspiration.*

To Gerald Cetrulo who reminded me of this book when it had gathered dust and I had forgotten about it.

And to Marty Meyer with constant sarcasm that never ceases to amaze me.

Robby & Rachel, With love and always in my thoughts, "Uncle Buck"

What is in the name ***portobello***? Not much— but this overgrown mushroom has a limitless number of possibilities. To the culinary imagination, its texture and ability to encompass my creativity have led me to gather my favorite recipes that you can easily prepare.

With seventeen years of practical experience as a chef I have had the opportunity to prepare all these and more dishes with the portobello.

From soups to steaks the flair added to an ordinary dish by the portobello is always mushrooming.

I hope you overwhelm your guests with the original recipes that follow.

— Ron Meyer

Before You Begin

A FEW WORDS ON
CLEANING THE MUSHROOM:
(A Simple Art)

The stem of the mushroom should snap off at the base of the cap (Figure 1).

For recipes calling for the use of the stem, cut off the dirty part of the stem and discard (Figure 2).

Using a teaspoon, scoop the black from the base of the mushroom cap (Figure 3).   Then clean gently with cold water.

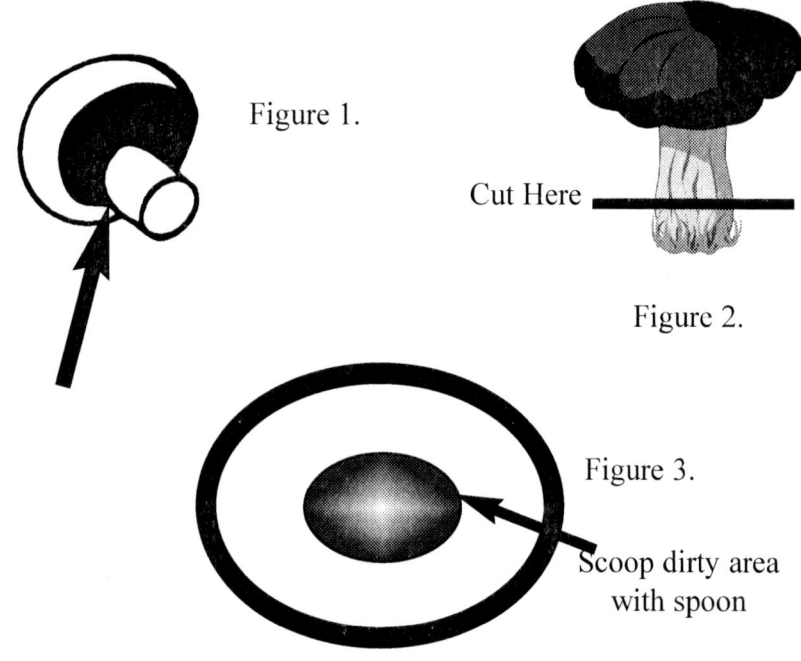

Figure 1.

Cut Here

Figure 2.

Figure 3.

Scoop dirty area
with spoon

PORTOBELLO MUSHROOM AND BARLEY SOUP
(yields approximately 1 gallon)

4 portobellos cleaned and destemmed
4 sprigs celery
1 carrot
1 white onion
1/4 cup chopped dill
1 tsp fresh chopped thyme
1 cup barley
1 quart chicken broth
1 quart beef broth
1 cup puree tomatoes
2 tsp brown sugar
salt and pepper to taste
1/4 cup extra virgin olive oil
1 bayleaf

Chop portobellos, carrots, celery and onion into small dice. In stock pot heat olive oil over medium heat. Add chopped vegetables and saute' until they start to soften. Then add chopped fine herbs (dill and thyme) toss and saute' for one minute. This will enable the herbs to release their flavor. Next add chicken and beef broth, puree tomatoes, brown sugar, salt, pepper and bay leaf and let simmer for 30 to 40 minutes. Add dry barley and cook for another 10 minutes until the barley is cooked and serve.

NOTE: The barley will absorb liquid as it sits in the soup. It is advised, if you wish ,to cook the barley separately and add it to the soup as you heat up the servings. You will prevent the barley from bloating.

Cooking Notes and My Personal Variations

PORTOBELLO AND BEEF KABOBS

1 lb beef cut into large cubes
1 onion
1 red pepper
1 yellow bell pepper
4 portobello mushrooms cleaned and destemmed

Marinade
1 cup red wine
1/4 cup soy sauce
1/4 cup worcestershire sauce
2 tsp brown sugar
1/2 cup olive oil
1 tsp salt and pepper
2 tsp fine herbs chopped (rosemary, thyme, dill etc.)

Cut onion, pepper, mushrooms and beef into large cubes. Marinate beef and mushroom in a large bowl with the above marinade ingredients and let sit for 1 hour. Thread steak, mushroom, pepper and onion onto skewer. Broil or grill kabobs 15 minutes until done. NOTE: Baste kabobs with marinate while cooking - every 3 or 4 minutes.

Cooking Notes and My Personal Variations

BEER BATTERED PORTOBELLO WITH ORANGE MARMALADE AND HORSERADISH DIPPING SAUCE

6 portobellos cleaned and destemmed
2 beers or ale
1 cup flour
1 tsp paprika
1 tsp salt
1 tsp pepper
1 tsp baking powder
1 jar orange marmalade
2 tsp white horseradish

Combine dry ingredients above and then mix with beer until you form a batter. Cut portobellos into large cubes. Dip in batter and fry in 375º oil until golden brown (approximately 3 minutes).

DIPPING MARMALADE

Combine marmalade and horseradish. Mix thoroughly.

Serve with toothpicks or small skewers for convenience

Cooking Notes and My Personal Variations

BLACKENED PORTOBELLO W/ROASTED PEPPER PUREE

6 portobellos - cleaned and destemmed
2 cups blackening spice(see below)
1 cup olive oil
6 whole red peppers
6 whole yellow bell peppers
top with garlic, salt and pepper to taste

BLACKENING SPICE

1/2 cup cayenne pepper
1/4 cup paprika
1 tblsp onion powder
1 tblsp garlic powder
1 tsp salt
1 tsp. black pepper

Add all ingredients together and mix thoroughly. Coat portobello with blackening spice to taste. The more you coat the spicier it will be. Heat olive oil in a pan till smoking. Add mushrooms and cook for 2 minutes on each side.

ROASTED PEPPERS

Coat pepper with olive oil and roast for 20 minutes at 400º. Turn to prevent burning every 10 minutes. Remove from oven and cover in foil and cool. Remove skin from peppers when cool. Separately puree peppers in a food processor. While peppers puree add 1 tsp garlic and 1 tsp of extra virgin olive oil, salt and pepper. Before serving warm puree in a small sauce pan.

To plate pour yellow and red puree on 1/2 a dish like a ying yang and serve mushrooms sliced over the top. Sear portobello mushroom in smoking hot oil until soft yet firm.

Cooking Notes and My Personal Variations

SAUTE' BROCCOLI RABE PORTOBELLOS WITH HOT CHERRY PEPPERS

2 heads chopped broccoli rabe
4 portobellos cleaned and destemmed
6 large cloves of garlic
1/4 cup extra virgin olive oil
1/4 cup sliced hot cherry peppers
salt and pepper to taste
1/4 cup chicken broth

Slice 6 cloves of garlic thinly. Slice portobellos into large thin strips. In large sauce pan heat olive oil over medium fire. Add garlic and brown. Then add chopped broccoli rabe and mushrooms. Toss and sauté. Add chicken stock, salt and pepper to taste. Cook until broccoli rabe is tender yet maintains a bright green vibrancy. Serve as a side dish or as a base with grilled chicken steak or shrimp.

Cooking Notes and My Personal Variations

GRILLED CHICKEN AND PORTOBELLO MUSHROOM CAESAR SALAD

3 portobellos cleaned and destemmed
3-6 to 8 oz. chicken breast
1 ear of corn
1 red onion
1/4 cup shredded carrots
1/2 cup Caesar salad dressing
1/4 cup grated parmesan cheese
1/4 cup croutons
1 head of chopped romaine lettuce
marinated portobello and chicken in marinade.
(see recipe used for the grilled marinated portobello on page 35.

On grill or broiler roast the chicken and mushrooms until cooked (approximately 8 minutes). Cut into large julienne strips and fan over Caesar salad. Sprinkle on corn(decobbed), carrots, onion, croutons and cheese. Serve on a chilled dish. Any Caesar salad mix will work fine. While tossing the chopped romaine incorporate cheese, croutons and dressing until all leaves are well coated.

Cooking Notes and My Personal Variations

_____

_____

_____

_____

_____

_____

_____

_____

_____

_____

_____

_____

_____

_____

_____

_____

_____

_____

_____

_____

_____

_____

_____

_____

_____

_____

<u>CHICKEN PORTOBELLO</u>

6 boneless breast of chicken
1 cup flour
2 tbsp butter
3 portobello mushrooms sliced
1/4 cup prosciutto
1/2 cup heavy cream
1 cup chicken stock
1/4 cup demigloss or beef broth
1 tsp truffle paste
salt and pepper to taste
1/4 cup corn oil
1 tsp shallots
1/4 cup apple jack

Dust chicken breast with flour. Heat skillet with olive oil. Add chicken breast and cook till light brown on each side. Add minced prosciutto, butter, sliced portobello, shallots and saute' until mushrooms start to soften. Flame with apple jack. Add heavy cream, chicken stock, demigloss, truffle paste, salt, pepper and butter. Reduce sauce till it starts to thicken. Plate chicken and spoon mushrooms atop the breast.

Cooking Notes and My Personal Variations

_____
_____
_____
_____
_____
_____

_____
_____
_____
_____
_____
_____
_____
_____
_____
_____
_____
_____
_____
_____
_____
_____
_____
_____
_____

CHICKEN AND PORTOBELLO STIRFRY
(Serves 4)

4 boneless chicken breasts 6 to 8 ounces
1 cup broccoli florets
1 cup snow peas
1 red pepper cut into julienne strips
3 portobello mushrooms cleaned and cut into julienne strips
1 pound cooked cappelini pasta
1 cup water chestnuts (canned will do fine)
Chicken Marinade

---

1 cup olive oil
1/2 cup soy sauce
1/2 cup terriaki sauce
1/2 teaspoon ground ginger
1 teaspoon fresh chopped dill
1 teaspoon course ground black pepper
2 bay leaves

In a small bowl mix 4 tablespoons cornstarch with equal parts cold water. Mix to form a smooth paste. In a large bowl combine all marinate ingredients. Cut chicken into large chunks and place into marinade. Let sit for 45 minutes to an hour. In a wok or large saute pan heat 3 teaspoons olive oil until smoking. Remove chicken from marinate and place into the smoking wok. Cook for two minutes stirring briskly and often. Add vegetables and toss for 1 minute. Pour in 1 cup of discarded marinate and simmer for 1 minute. Slowly pour in corn starch mixture until you achieve the desired consistency. Serve stirfry over chilled noodles. Garnish with fresh chopped dill.

Cooking Notes and My Personal Variations

PORTOBELLO COMPANARE

6-6" diameter destemmed and cored mushrooms
2 eggplants
1 zucchini
1 yellow squash
1/4 lb. sliced mozzarella
1/2 cup gaeta olives
1 small red onion
1 cup prepared marinara sauce
pinch of salt and pepper
1/2 cup extra virgin olive oil

Cut eggplant, zucchini, yellow squash and red onion to medium dice. In saute' pan heat olive oil and brown garlic. Add vegetables and olive oil and cook until the mixture starts to soften. Add prepared grated cheese and marinara sauce. Cook for 3 minutes. Remove from the stove and chill the mixture. Scoop mix into portobello caps and bake for 10-12 minutes at 375°. Top the mushroom with mozzarella and brown cheese serve on heated dish.

Cooking Notes and My Personal Variations

5 LAYER STUFFED PORTOBELLO

6 portobello mushrooms capped and destemmed
1/4 lb thinly sliced prosciutto
1 lb red roasted peppers
1/2 lb sliced mozzarella cheese
1/2 lb goat cheese
1 tsp salt
1 tsp pepper
1/4 cup grated parmesan cheese
1/4 cup extra virgin olive oil

In cleaned portobello mushroom cap layer ingredients in as follows: Prosciutto, cheese, red roasted peppers and sliced mozzarella. Sprinkle with salt, pepper and parmesan. Drizzle on olive oil and bake for 12-15 minutes at 375 º

Cooking Notes and My Personal Variations

PORTOBELLO WITH EGGPLANT, PROSCIUTTO, GOAT CHEESE, AND BUFFALO MOZZARELLA

27 portobellos destemmed and cored
1 sliced eggplant
1/2 lb thinly sliced prosciutto
1/2 lb goat cheese
1 lb buffalo mozzarella
6 eggs
1/2 cup grated parmesan and romano cheese
1 cup corn oil
pinch salt and pepper

Thinly slice eggplant. Crack eggs and make egg wash with 1/4 cup of grated cheese. Dredge eggplant in eggwash and fry in corn oil. Remove from pan and cool. Layer in portobello, eggplant, prosciutto, goat cheese then buffalo mozzarella. Sprinkle with grated cheese and bake for 12 minutes at 325º. Great when served over a bed of pesto cream sauce.

Cooking Notes and My Personal Variations

PORTOBELLO FAJITAS

4 portobellos cleaned and destemmed
10 flour tortillas
1 large onion
1 green pepper
1 red pepper
1 tsp soy sauce
1 tsp lemon
1 tsp worcestershire sauce

Cut mushroom onion and pepper into julienne strips.   In a smoking hot saute' pan or preferably a cast iron skillet pan sear mushroom onion and peppers for 2 minutes. Add soy sauce, lemon and worcestershire sauce. Toss and remove from heat. To heat tortillas preheat oven to 375º and place tortillas on baking sheet and heat in oven for one minute.

FAJITA FIXINGS

1 cup shredded lettuce
1/4 cup shredded cheddar cheese
3 sliced jalapenos
1/4 cup diced tomatoes
1/4 cup guacamole
1/4 cup sour cream

On bed of shredded lettuce arrange above ingredients in separate yet distinguishable piles.

Cooking Notes and My Personal Variations

PORTOBELLO FINGERS

6 Portobellos destemmed and cleaned
6 eggs
1/2 cup flour
2 cups seasoned bread crumbs
1/2 cup grated cheese (romano and or parmesan)

Cut mushrooms into thick strips. Dredge in flour.
Dip in eggwash and then bread crumbs until well coated.
Fry in 375º oil until golden brown

Eggwash
6 eggs beaten with 1/2 cup grated cheese

Serve with marinara dipping sauce

Cooking Notes and My Personal Variations

FRESH SHRIMP AND PORTOBELLO STIRFRY (Serves 4)

1 pound fresh shrimp peeled and devained
1 cup snow peas
1 yellow bell pepper julienne cut
1 cup fresh broccoli florets
1 sliced carrot
1 cup water chestnuts (canned will do fine)
4 cups cooked white rice
2 teaspoons butter
Stirfry Sauce

Mix all ingredients:
1 cup white wine
1/4 cup lemon juice
1 teaspoon fresh chopped dill
1 teaspoon fresh chopped thyme (lemon thyme if available)
1/2 cup clam juice

In a small bowl mix 4 tablespoons cornstarch with equal part cold water. Mix together and form a smooth paste.
In a wok or large saute pan heat butter over medium high heat. Add shrimp and all vegetables and toss briskly while sauteing for 2 to 3 minutes until shrimp are about 75% cooked. Add stirfry sauce and continue to cook for 3 minutes. Slowly pour in cornstarch to achieve desired consistency. Serve stirfry over cooked white rice in a slightly heated bowl or plate.

Cooking Notes and My Personal Variations

GRILLED MARINATED PORTOBELLO

Portobello Marinade
equal parts
2 cups olive oil
2 cups balsamic vinegar
chopped rosemary, thyme (equivalent to 2 tsp)
1 squeezed lemon
1 tsp salt
1 tsp pepper - black course grind
6 stemmed and cored portobello caps
Marinate 2 to 3 hours

Grill marinated mushrooms until soft yet still with some firmness and plate. Serve topped with browned garlic in olive oil.

Grilled marinated portobello mushrooms are delicious when served over a fine New York Steak. See page 73 for suggestions on selection of a perfect cut.

Cooking Notes and My Personal Variations

MIXED FIELD GREEN SALAD TOPPED WITH GRILLED PORTOBELLO MUSHROOM WITH GARLIC AND BALSAMIC DRESSING

Field greens: or mesculin salad are organically grown baby let-tuces. Their crisp taste and a beautiful array of color makes the simplest salad special.

Using the marinated portobello mushroom recipe: take mushroom and grill until tender yet still with some firmness. Cut and fan mushroom on top of plate of mesculin greens.

Dressing:

6 garlic cloves
1/2 cup extra virgin olive oil
1/4 cup balsamic vinegar
tblsp sugar
tblsp soy sauce
tsp salt
tsp pepper

Heat oil in saute' pan until smoking. Brown garlic in oil and add balsamic vinegar, soy sauce, salt, pepper and sugar and reduce sauce slightly. Pour over mushroom and greens.

Cooking Notes and My Personal Variations

PORTOBELLO WITH GOAT CHEESE AND HERBS

6 portobello caps
1 lb. goat cheese
1 egg
dill, rosemary, thyme, parsley and chives-chopped salt and pepper to taste

Mix egg, goat cheese, salt, pepper and spices. Fill mushrooms and bake for 10 minutes at 400º. Serve with herb infused olive oil. Drizzle over the top.

Cooking Notes and My Personal Variations

PORTOBELLO MASHED POTATOES

6 large white potatoes
4 portobellos
1/2 lb butter
1 tsp garlic
1 tsp shallots
salt and pepper to taste
1/4 cup heavy cream
1/4 cup extra virgin olive oil
1 tsp truffle paste (optional)

Peel 6 large potatoes and boil until mashable then mash. Clean and destem portobellos. Cut the mushroom into small cubes and saute' in olive oil with garlic and shallots. When the mushrooms are softened add butter, salt, pepper and heavy cream. Simmer for 2 to 3 minutes. Add mushroom mixture to mashed potatoes and mix thoroughly. You might need to add extra heavy cream to attain desired consistency.

NOTE: Truffle paste can be added to give this recipe a more eclectic flair. It adds intense mushroom flavor.

Cooking Notes and My Personal Variations

_____

_____

_____

_____

_____

_____

_____

_____

_____

_____

_____

_____

_____

_____

_____

_____

_____

_____

_____

_____

_____

_____

_____

_____

_____

3 EGG PORTOBELLO OMELETTE

3 eggs
1 portobello cleaned and destemmed
1/4 cup heavy cream
pinch salt and pepper
2 tblsp butter
1 tsp grated cheese

Beat eggs with heavy cream, salt, pepper and grated cheese. Thinly slice the mushroom and saute' in teflon pan with butter. When the mushroom starts to soften add eggs and continue to cook until the eggs are done. Flip omelette and serve.

NOTE: Add swiss cheese or sharp shredded cheddar cheese for a heartier omelette.

Cooking Notes and My Personal Variations

PORTOBELLO PARMESAN

6 portobellos cleaned and destemmed
6 eggs
1/4 cup corn oil
1 cup parmesan cheese
1 quart prepared marinara sauce
3 cups seasoned bread crumbs
1/2 lb sliced mozzarella cheese
2 tblsp dry basil

Prepare eggwash by beating 6 eggs and 1/4 cup parmesan cheese. Bread the mushroom caps by dipping the cap first in eggwash then into the bread crumbs. Make sure the mushroom is well coated with the bread crumbs. In saute' pan heat oil until smoking. Fry the mushroom in oil until golden brown on each side. On baking sheet place the cooked mushrooms and top with marinara sauce, parmesan cheese and sprinkle with dry basil. Top with mozzarella cheese and bake for 7 to 10 minutes at 350º. Serve with pasta to make a great vegetarian Italian dinner.

Cooking Notes and My Personal Variations

PENNE PASTA WITH PORTOBELLO MUSH-ROOMS AND PLUM TOMATO SAUCE

1 lb dry penne pasta
6 portobello mushrooms cleaned and destemmed
1/4 cup extra virgin olive oil
2 tsp minced garlic
32oz canned plum tomatoes
1/4 cup chopped fresh basil
1 tsp salt
1 tsp pepper
1/4 cup grated parmesan cheese

In pasta pot boil 3 quarts of water with 2 tsp salt. Add dry pasta when water achieves a rolling boil. Cook until al dente (approximately 8-10 minutes). Drain and hold. In separate sauce pan heat olive oil over medium fire. Add garlic and brown, then add sliced mushrooms and saute' until slightly tender. Add plum tomatoes, (which have been crushed either by hand or in a food processor), basil, salt and pepper. Let simmer for 5-8 minutes. Pour sauce over cooked pasta and toss with grated cheese then serve.

Cooking Notes and My Personal Variations

PORTOBELLO STUFFED WITH VEAL AND PINE NUTS

6 Portobellos cleaned and destemmed
1 lb ground veal
1 cup pine nuts
1 egg
1/4 cup grated parmesan cheese
1/4 cup bread crumbs
1 tsp salt
1 tsp pepper
1 tsp ground garlic
1 tsp oregano
1 tsp basil
1 tbsp tomato puree
1 tbsp olive oil

Brown pine nuts in oil until lightly brown. Combine all ingredients. Fill portobello with meat mixture and bake for 20 minutes at 375°. Serve with marinara sauce.

Cooking Notes and My Personal Variations

PORTOBELLO PIZZA

1 pre-cooked pizza crust
1/2 cup prepared marinara sauce
1/2 cup shredded mozzarella cheese
1/4 cup grated parmesan romano mixture
2 portobello mushrooms
pinch salt, pepper, and oregano
1/4 cup chopped fresh basil
1/4 cup olive oil

Clean and cut portobello into long thin strips. In saute' pan heat olive oil and cook the mushroom for 1 minute. Remove from pan and drain excess oil from mushroom. Sprinkle with salt and pepper.

On prepared pie crust, ladle and spread marinara sauce evenly. Sprinkle on mozzarella and grated cheeses. Distribute portobello evenly on pizza. Sprinkle on oregano and bake in preheated oven at 475º for 10-13 minutes until crust is golden brown.

Cooking Notes and My Personal Variations

PORTOBELLO WRAP HORS DOEUVRE'S

6 portobellos cleaned and destemmed
1 lb lean bacon
2 tsp minced garlic
1/4 cup extra virgin olive oil
2 tsp fine herbs
pinch of salt and pepper

Combine oil, garlic, fine herbs, salt and pepper. Cut portobellos into 1/2" cubes. Wrap mushroom with bacon. Drizzle garlic olive oil herb mixture and bake until bacon is crisp and mushroom tenderizes. Approximately 10 minutes at 375°

Cooking Notes and My Personal Variations

PORTOBELLO QUICHE

1 pie crust
3 sliced portobello mushroom caps
6 eggs
1/2 cup heavy cream
1 tsp salt and pepper
1/2 cup shredded swiss cheese
1 tsp chopped parsley
1 tsp paprika
1 tsp butter

Slice portobello caps thinly and saute' in butter until tender (about 2 minutes). Beat eggs, heavy cream, salt and pepper. Place portobellos in bottom of pie crust.   Sprinkle in the shredded swiss cheese. Slowly pour in the egg mixture until shell is 3/4 full. Bake in 375º oven for 20-25 minutes until about 80% cooked. Sprinkle on parsley and then paprika for color. Cook until firm and remove from oven and cool. It is much easier to slice when the quiche has cooled and set.

Cooking Notes and My Personal Variations

PORTOBELLO MUSHROOM RISOTTO

3 portobellos cleaned and destemmed
2 cup precooked risotto
2 tblsp butter
1/4 cup grated parmesan cheese
1 tsp shallots
1/4 cup brandy
1/4 cup heavy cream
1 tsp truffle paste
salt and pepper to taste

Slice portobellos into julienne strips and then cut them in half. In saute' pan heat butter and shallots. As the shallots start to brown add mushrooms and saute' for 1 minute. Flame with brandy and cook until the liquid evaporates. Add precooked risotto, heavy cream, salt, pepper, cheese and truffle paste. Toss rice and mushroom mixture until 90% of the liquid is absorbed and the risotto has a creamy consistency. On heated dish spoon out risotto and garnish with chopped parsley and serve.

NOTE: To cook risotto follow instructions on the package. To add extra flavor use white wine when cooking the rice. The risotto will absorb the flavor of the wine and the result will be a sweeter tangier product.

Cooking Notes and My Personal Variations

_____

_____

_____

_____

_____

_____

_____

_____

_____

_____

_____

_____

_____

_____

_____

_____

_____

_____

_____

_____

_____

_____

_____

_____

_____

_____

PORTOBELLO WITH SAUSAGE AND SAGE STUFFING

6-6" portobellos, destemmed and cored
1 lb cooked chopped Italian sausage
2 tsp chopped sage
2 cups seasoned bread crumbs
1/4 cup parmesan and romano cheese
1/4 cup olive oil

Combine cooked Italian sausage with drippings, sage, bread crumbs and cheese mix thoroughly stuff mushroom and drizzle with olive oil. Bake 15 minutes at 375°. Can be served over bachemel sauce or marinara for added flair.

Cooking Notes and My Personal Variations

PORTOBELLO WITH
SAUTEED' SCALLOPS

6 portobellos cleaned and destemmed
1 lb bay scallops
2 tbsp butter
1 cup heavy cream
1/2 cup seafood stock (clam juice will do)
1 tsp shallots
1 tsp lemon thyme
1/2 cup brandy
1 tsp parsley
salt and pepper to taste

Saute' scallops in butter for 2 to 3 minutes with shallots. Flame with brandy. Cook until the alcohol cooks out. Add lemon thyme, salt and pepper and coat scallops by tossing briskly in pan. Add seafood stock and heavy cream and reduce until the sauce has a creamy consistency. Bake portobellos in the oven at 375º for 10 minutes until tender (al dente) Plate portobellos and spoon scallop mixture over the top of mushrooms. Garnish with chopped parsley and a sprig of lemon thyme.

Cooking Notes and My Personal Variations

SEAFOOD STUFFED PORTOBELLOS

6-6" diameter portobellos destemmed and cored
1/2 cup chopped cooked shrimp
1/2 cup crabmeat (or sea legs imitation)
2 eggs
1 tsp shallots
1 tsp mustard
1 tsp mayonnaise
pinch of salt, pepper and old bay seasoning

Combine above ingredients to form a loose batter like mixture. Stuff mushroom and let bake for 15-20 minutes at 375º. When filling has a quiche like consistency sprinkle with parsley and paprika and serve.

Cooking Notes and My Personal Variations

PORTOBELLOS WITH A SHERRY MUSHROOM FILLING

6 portobello tops
6 portobello stems
1 lb ricotta cheese
1 egg
2 cups sherry wine
1/2 tsp shallots
pinch of salt and pepper
2 tabls butter
1 cup chicken stock

Dice portobello stems into small pieces. Saute' stems in melted butter with shallots, salt and pepper until soft. Flame with sherry and add chicken stock. Reduce until all the liquid is absorbed and chill. Add mushroom mixture to cheese and egg. Bake 10 minutes at 375° and serve.

Cooking Notes and My Personal Variations

CREAM OF PORTOBELLO MUSHROOM SOUP
(yields approximately 1 gallon)

6 portobello mushrooms with stems
1/2 cup butter
1/2 cup flour
1 qt. heavy cream
3 qts. chicken stock
1 tbsp. salt
1 tsp pepper
1 tbsp minced garlic
1 tbsp minced shallots
1 cup marsala or sherry wine
2 bay leaves
1 tsp nutmeg
1/4 cup cornstarch if needed

Clean black from underneath mushroom cap. Cut caps and stems into large yet thin slices. In stock pot saute' cut mushrooms, shallots and garlic in 1/2 cup butter until soft. Add flour to make a rue. Cook for 2 minutes and flame with marsala or sherry wine. Add chicken stock, heavy cream and remainder of ingredients. Cook until soup reaches slow boil and thickens. If extra thickening is needed use cornstarch sluree to the mixture to add extra thickening.

Cooking Notes and My Personal Variations

PORTOBELLO STUFFED WITH SPANISH RICE AND CHICKEN

6 portobello caps destemmed and cored
1 cup cooked rice
3 cups chicken broth
2 tsp olive oil
1/4 cup chopped scallions
1/4 cup diced tomatoes
1/4 cup diced green and red pepper
1/2 cup diced cooked chicken
1 tblsp tomato paste
3 tsp chopped minced onions
salt and pepper to taste
1 tsp minced cilantro

Saute' white rice with minced onions and olive oil for 1 minute. Add chicken broth and cover. Cook until the broth is about 3/4 absorbed in the rice (about 8 minutes). Add diced chicken, tomatoes, scallions, peppers, salt, pepper, cilantro and tomato paste. Cook until all the liquid is absorbed and chill. Stuff portobello caps and bake for 12-15 minutes at 375°.

Serve over salsa garnished with cilantro and diced red and green peppers.

Cooking Notes and My Personal Variations

SPICY PORTOBELLO MUSHROOM AND ONION SAUTE'

3 sliced portobellos cleaned and destemmed
2 medium white onions
2 tbsp butter
1 bottle ketchup
1/4 cup lemon juice
2 tsp red pepper flakes

Saute' mushrooms and onions in butter until tender. Add red pepper flakes, lemon juice and ketchup. Cook until onions carmalize and you get a thick saucy consistency.

Cooking Notes and My Personal Variations

NEW YORK STEAK WITH MARINATED PORTOBELLO MUSHROOM

Choosing a fine steak for a meal is choice. The best steak cannot be chosen on price alone. You get what you pay for. Broil or grill your steak to desired temperature. Then after using the marinated mushroom recipe from page 35 cut on a bias and place over top of the finished steak.

Cooking Notes and My Personal Variations

PORTOBELLO AND TENDERLOIN STIRFRY

3 sliced portobello mushrooms
1 lb slice beef tenderloin
1 red bell pepper
1 yellow bell pepper
1 small onion
1 head broccoli
1 cup snow peas
1 tbsp olive oil

Stirfry Sauce

1/2 cup beef broth
3 tablespoons soy sauce
1/2 tsp ground ginger
1 tsp salt and pepper
2 tbsp corn starch

Cut beef, mushrooms and vegetables into julienne strips. In smoking hot wok or sauté pan heat oil. Add beef and brown then add all vegetables. Stir fry for 2 minutes. Stir in broth mixture and cook another 2 minutes. Thicken with corn starch sluree until you reach the desired thickness. Serve over rice or broad noodles.

Cooking Notes and My Personal Variations

PORTOBELLO FLORENTINE

6 portobellos-about 6" diameter
1 cup ricotta cheese
2 tblsp parmesan ricotta cheese (grated)
1/2 cup chopped spinach
pinch salt and pepper
1 tsp shallots
1 egg
1 cup seasoned bread crumbs

Destem the portobello and cut away the black inside leaving a small rim on the outside edge of the mushroom when preparing all stuffed portobellos.

Mix the cheeses, egg, spinach, shallots, salt and pepper thoroughly. Stuff the cored mushroom with the above mixture with a rubber spatula leaving a smooth texture to the stuffed portobello. Sprinkle on bread crumbs and brown under broiler until the mushroom is tender (about 8-12 minutes).

Cooking Notes and My Personal Variations

_____

_____

_____

_____

_____

_____

_____

_____

_____

_____

_____

_____

_____

_____

_____

_____

_____

_____

_____

_____

_____

_____

_____

_____

_____

_____

_____

_____

PORTOBELLO WITH 5 CHEESE STUFFING

6 portobello caps cleaned
1 qt. ricotta cheese
1/2 lb. chopped shredded mozzarella cheese
1 cup shredded provolone
1/4 cup grated romano cheese
1/4 cup grated parmesan cheese
1 egg
1 tablespoon minced shallot
salt and pepper to taste
1 cup seasoned bread crumbs

Combine ricotta, mozzarella, provolone, romano, and parmesan cheese. Mix in egg, salt, pepper and shallots thoroughly. In cleaned portobello mushroom cap spoon in filling. Bake for 15 minutes at 350°. Sprinkle finished product with seasoned bread crumbs and brown under the broiler. Be careful not to burn the crumbs. Serve over marinara sauce on a heated dish.

Cooking Notes and My Personal Variations

PORTOBELLO WITH SUNDRIED TOMATOES AND RICOTTA STUFFING

6-6" diameter portobellos destemmed and cored
1 cup ricotta cheese
1/2 cup chopped sundried tomatoes
1/4 cup ricotta parmesan grated cheese
1 egg
1 tsp shallots
1/2 cup chopped mozzarella cheese
pinch salt and pepper
seasoned bread crumbs
1/4 cup chopped basil

Combine above ingredients and stuff cored mushroom. Dip in seasoned bread crumbs and bake 10-12 minutes at 375°. Serve with a drizzle of sundried tomato infused olive oil.

Cooking Notes and My Personal Variations

_____
_____
_____
_____
_____
_____
_____
_____
_____
_____
_____
_____
_____
_____
_____
_____
_____
_____
_____
_____
_____
_____
_____
_____
_____
_____
_____
_____

BROILED VEAL CHOP WITH PORTOBELLOS, PEPPERS AND MUSHROOMS

4-2" thick loin veal chops
6 portobellos cleaned and destemmed
1 large white onion
1 tsp sliced garlic
2 red bell peppers
2 yellow bell peppers
1/4 cup extra virgin olive oil
tsp salt and pepper
tsp dry oregano
1/4 cup balsamic vinegar

Broil veal chops to desired temperature. Slice portobello thinly. Slice onion and cube bell peppers. Heat olive oil until smoking. Add garlic, onions, peppers and mushrooms. Saute' for 2 minutes until the contents start to soften and carmalized. Add salt, pepper and oregano and toss. Deglaze with balsamic vinegar and pour over top of veal chops and serve.

Other Cooking Terms I've learned

TERMS TO FAMILIARIZE WITH:

Al Dente   -   to cook firm yet tender

Bechamel sauce   -   a cream sauce with nut-
                                              meg, salt and pepper.

Blacking   -   to coat food with spice or
cajun spice and cooking highly heated oil

Carmalize   -   to saute' till golden brown

Deglaze   -   to render flavor of a pan
                                              you have cooked with
                           by adding liquid to lift the flavor

Dice   -   to cut into small cubes

Dredge   -   to cover in flour or batter

Drippings   -   the fat left in the pan after
                                              cooking. Has great flavor!

Drizzle   -   to drip sauce or oil over
                                              food

Eggwash   -   beaten eggs with salt, pep-
                                              per and grated cheese

FAN   -   to cut and display in a fan-
                                              like design
Fine Herbs   -fine chopped herbs - any mixture

Other Cooking Terms I've Learned

_____

_____

_____

_____

_____

_____

_____

_____

_____

_____

_____

_____

_____

_____

_____

_____

_____

_____

_____

_____

_____

_____

_____

_____

Flame   -   to cook with alcohol.
                                                    Flaming eliminates
                              alcohol yet leaves flavor of the liquor

Julienne   -   to cut into long thin strips

Mince   -   to cut into small pieces
                                                            with a knife

Puree   -   pulped fruit or vegetable
                              cooked and passed through a sieve

Reduce   -   to cook a sauce so that much of
                                                    the liquid evaporates

Roux   -   equal parts butter and flour
                                                        cooked together
                                                and use to thicken soups
                                                            and sauces

Saute   -   to fry quickly in small
                                                          amount of oil

Seasoned flour   -   flour with seasonings such
                                                        as salt and pepper

Sluree   -   a paste made from corn
                                                starch and cold water.
                                                Use to thicken sauces

Other Mushroom Recipes I've Found

Other Mushroom Recipes I've Found